Everyone I've Danced With Is Dead.

Mamie Morgan

JACKLEG PRESS

Praise for *Everyone I've Danced With Is Dead.*

Reading these poems is like sitting down with a friend for a conversation – the kind of friend you trust to tell all of the truth, but with mercy. These whip-smart poems don't flinch, even at the hardest truths about what it means to be human – to love and to lose, to damage and be damaged, to live through moments "where the quake originates," that make you cling to "every word that had ever made me want to stay alive." These poems have an electric power, one strong enough to change lives. Morgan faces devastation with such an open grace and generosity that a reader can't help but feel there's one truth more real than any other: that even in the moments that shake us to the core, there is always hope.

—Emma Bolden

I'm not sure anymore who's the main character...," Morgan says in one poem. And, indeed, in this exceptional, fiercely humane book, characters and stories blend fluidly one into another. These are fast-talking poems, with surprising pacing and unpredictable run-on syntax, yet somehow remain plaintive and soulful. They are deeply imaginative portraits of dislocation that swerve through the realities of life--fear, anger, angst, troubling politics--yet somehow seem celebratory. I enjoyed this book immensely. I know I am reading the real thing when it makes me want to get to my desk and back to work on my own art. *Everyone I've Danced With Is Dead* is the real thing.

—Mark Cox

The central organ pumping blood through these poems is wonderment. Morgan's particular brand of wonder knows no hierarchies: love, betrayal, fallings out, quotidian, joy, jail, sex, school, the body, war, race, politics, and that old tricker Death all crowd around the same table. This book pulls you forward and shows you the world as it is--a mess worth celebrating, recoiling from, enduring, and embracing. These poems are built of risk and witness--importantly, they have the language and daring to match. This is one helluva barn burner.
—Michael McGriff

JackLeg Press
www.jacklegpress.org

ISBN: 978-1956907070

Library of Congress Control Number: 2023945613

Cover design by Simone Muench.
Author photo by Will Crooks.

Contents

Three

Acknowledgments   61

for Kirby, and for Patrick

But if I never do nothing
I'll get you back some day.

—Tom Petty

Poetry is like seeing Pirates of the Caribbean
when you're not ready for it. When you're small.
When you're, like, seven.

—Brian Joye

Everyone I've Danced With Is Dead.

B's failing poetry, but he's a nice boy,
lives in his leather bomber, loves AP Bio,

is cool to no one.
      When he leans against

the hand-me-down Ikea chaise
in my office, says *it feels like a valley,*

      were a valley everywhere,
I make him a copy

of some Simic poem about Euclid
& chickens & light-dressed women carrying

parasols & Saturday morning
      before they find him I dress

in a black gown with cut-outs careful
to keep the tags intact for a pageant

      I've entered at some Baptist church.
My dad carries a sickness so small

in his merkel cells we haven't met it yet.

Everything's a joke.

For weeks my boyfriend Josh & I practice
      our show walk up & down the carport,

smoking ladylike the both of us over a trill
of my school-issued iPad's *Toddlers & Tiaras.*

       Josh's casual walk is killer. It's 2013.
I don't remember anything else

that whole year. I hear Josh is a welder now
& has like a hundred babies.

       I bet he's burned
so many things back together.

One

Letter to Yasha In My Third Period AP Lang Class, Morning After That Girl She Likes Blocked Her On Instagram

There must be something that can fix me,
you say, but in sixteen years nothing has. Lexapro,

Oleptro, Thiopropazate. Eighth grade, Hal Stoddard
chased me into the Rosewood Lane cul-de-sac by the butt-end

of his BB gun yelling, *C'mon piggy-piggy, open up you whale,*
while I recited every word that had ever made me want to stay alive:

supine, rocking chair, sherbet, mother, diphthong, Halloween
carnival, far-off longed-for spinsterdom. I don't know what to say

the grown folks you don't listen to haven't already said. Celexa, Paxil,
Luvox, not all days will suck. I've a pitbull & a brick home & there comes

an age people stop minding you so much, leave you well enough
alone. Hal came back, brandishing carnations, asked could I play

H-O-R-S-E in Ben Nixon's driveway some few houses down, asked
if I'd like to see John Lennon in concert come summer. Course I did.

Lennon's dead, he laughed, *you stupid cunt,* & allowed that basketball
to roll into the woods where we sometimes hid together as children.

Who knows why I'm telling you this, years later before the doctor
took out what was no longer alive, last thing I saw before the drugs

set in was a poster of tulips in a Dutch paddock taped to the ceiling.
Just after, my mother drew a warm bath, put me in it, fed

us oysters & albariño. Things fall away like a tilt of roadway to unearth
twenty years of soon-to-flower field. My mother allowed me to utter

oyster until I fell into a wing of sleep. There are minutes, *Yasha, Yasha,*
I like to imagine the baby lived, that a word was so loved she'd

travel the earth by train or foot or tippytoe
                                repeating it, just repeating it.

Everyone I've Danced With Is Dead.

I don't know how to build the world
I've asked you to build, how to write him
taking you hood-up against the engine

of his Pontiac without sending your poem
into some country song of a Saint Tammany
Parish childhood you can never get back.

One winter our father bought our mother
a hatbox of lingerie including her first thong
& she spent that grace-note of Christmas

buck-dancing through the living room
like some blown-hoofed mule, those hunter
green drawers upholstered to her head.

What else is a woman to do after the man
she's known twenty years puts to her the task
of reimagining their own life? She sent him

receipt in hand back to the drawing board
of stores confused. She sent him out into
the earth like a fool. I don't know why people

act the way they do, but one night in hospice
my dad dreams he's a Brazilian painting &
afterward Mom climbs into his bed saying:

> Show me
> what you look like.

Everyone I've Danced With Is Dead.

The students have written about birds
because I've suggested heartbreak,

the loss of a farm, some senior
named Marcus sending all your private texts

to the group—any of it is capture, migration.

Farrah's parents just split, which in any other class
wouldn't be anybody's business.

But this is poetry:
        her dad driving that delusion of motorcycle
        & refusing to pay for anything.

        How about jackdaws falling

into the small production
of a quiet country
no one has seen?

How about the hummingbirds
for whom my father demanded

        clear sightlines as he died?

What about the girl I loved
who dropped a nest full of chicks

from her third story

hospital room

& fucking laughed.

About Drowning

How only in dreams the lady writes
beautiful poems where her mother can fly

but then again so can everyone else
        so still she's unable to find her.

How some of us invent ourselves
as witches, since no one hunts

        witches anymore.

Or we hide inside the stuffed doll of time, & are
mostly thankful.

Dreams, always a jotted down magic
supply store of our own accidental making:

He's a shepherd. A bad one
but a shepherd still. Couldn't,

in fact,

shepherd in his sleep
& yet it rains always
at the right time

on his side of the road.
Luck not the fame any kid
hopes for.

Of course she knows what it means;
she's a teacher. She suggests they write

a poem including algae, forgiveness, the liver.
They ask why, & she doesn't know.

Sixteen & wrapped in a bridesmaid's dress
lavender as eye shadow she snuck a smoke

at her sister's wedding reception.
From the bushes she saw their father

steal back a bag phone from the bride's
Honda, this only thing left he owned of her,

   which is where the quake originates.

I'm not sure anymore who's the main character,
who's the sister, who is me.

Their father kept his office door open
so all the coeds could hear his music.

Under the criticism section
of his annual evaluation, her

department chair writes, firm as his job:

Social.

Which in any other language looks like a mother
flinging every street-facing window open,
searching for more mothers.

When the writing students ask for advice
she suggests they sell tractor supply.

When they ask about teaching
she suggests guiding rivers.

When her mother calls she wonders
why no one ever warned her about drowning,

      about being drowned.

Everyone I've Danced With Is Dead.

In Ouray, Colorado, this farmer puts out
a basket of hedge apples each morning
for the doe living in his back land. Except

one day he doesn't & the doe, she walks
right up to his back door, jiggles the knob
with her teeth. It's every girl for herself

before sun-up. There's the he who is going
& the she who remains, the entire springs
that pass into autumns, Jefferson, Georgia,

where trucks traffic crates of chickens
into this or that hell & a woman arrives
at her driveway's end, lifts those fallen

unfastened from the back. *It happens,*
you write, *more than anyone would like
to think.* You can't get any of it right

because the driveway woman is your mom
& all workshop wants is an explanation:
How many die, how many live. I've never

gotten what I want from the doe & I've been
writing that poem forever. Some limb of our
soul never understands what hay it's hauling.

Everyone I've Danced With Is Dead.

Hours before they identify him Garrett DM's me
the recipe for perfect eggplant parm:

Everyone knows, he begins, *you salt the skin.*

When the visions started they started small, so you couldn't tell:

was it skag or too much brown liquor
or maybe left entirely alone

the banisters of his mind filled
        during a matinee of long days
                between jobs.

Everyone knows you slice lengthwise.

Garrett's duplex so short a drive from mine
that when he called I often showed up barefoot

& purseless, often flinched at the sound
of my own finger tapping his glass door.

All you need to know is the last time,

a gaucho knife he clutched above the fox—
        brown, dead, small as a leather loafer

my dad used to beat down
a roach or wasp's nest from any wall.

Whether he found it,

whether he killed it,
              whether Garrett
put it out some misery never mattered. I never asked.

You can tell grown folks are about to go
when they begin to look like kids again.

The trick, he says, *is sauce,*
& I imagine him typing
into his Galaxy both-handed,

a Newport buoyed against the still lake of his lip.
Use half what they tell you, maybe half of half,

& I assume by they he means our grandmothers
          & the women we called our grandmothers

who weren't any kin but helped

      in cleaning us up,
              beating us good,
                      shipping us out.

(Maybe what you need to know is how we met:

Summer after fourth grade at sleepaway camp
named for Cherokees though every last counselor
was white, ours a teen who wore shark's teeth around
his neck & looked nearly like a grown man or god, who
once as punishment dropped Garrett & me in the middle

of Agowatiha Forest for days with only one apple,
said, *Take this, eat it core & stem, don't think
of coming back till there's nothing left of you.*)

Bail

I.

Here it is all those years ago the night

      Officer Talbron pushes me past
            the neighbor's broken marigold pot

& into the moral hush of his patrol car.
      Here is the lion not letting go I haven't been

      in years, the drunk, the closed canyon
            of a mouth whose friends turn up

long dead, long buried the most of them
      behind a Regal theater up Fernwood.

      Sometimes my student Emilia falls
            into the prison of her own sleep

& can still hear the cell slam of her mother
      into nothing, can still conjure the root

      system of her Cuban home, sometimes
            from across the room I can find her

through the arresting lens of grief's old engine
      turning this or that corner onto a street

      she no longer recognizes, riding for not
            the first time this long makeshift raft

of truancy, where at some point even our own
      bodies become a vanishing point none of us

      can recover.

II.

In jail, you see all sorts of things:

      turpentine opaquing its army
          down the width of a forearm,

angels, entire stories—
      the one about a litter of treeing Pit bulls sliced

      from their still-breathing mother,
          that one from somebody's Bible.

But not everything is sad.

      I once knew a bunch of girls
          who broke free with only a wrench,

somebody's molars, somebody's bartered-for
      bundle of string.

First Day (August, 2005)

Vomit in the house.
A red Solo cup
tossed in the yard.
            —Martin, haiku assignment

I warn the college kids against writing
about being wasted, that being wasted

is fine, though the lack of specificity
troublesome as a broken cork

in some bottle of Sangiovese
at the start of a very bad first date,

when I wouldn't wish sobriety
upon them or anyone. I'm referring

to Martin but saying *class*
the way we disguise ourselves

as who we partially are. As a little girl
I assumed New Orleans an island,

that getting there you were expected
to behave and wear stockings.

Grandmother Polly seemed to fern
her way across The Pontchartrain—

queen of the perished, her parishioners.
Stacked alongside women brandishing

peacock-feathered hats & visiting, later,
Aunt Gladys while she styled the manes

of poodles & other Cuban ladies
who delivered us kids boxes of beads,

cohitos dangling from their mouths.
You see? There are no islands anyone

can't get to, we grow up reading
from some faraway place about

the twenty-two who tied themselves
together with clothesline downtown,

the slurring storm killing them
anyway. Not like queens, or even people,

like bowling pins in some Alabamian
Star Lanes. The wasted. Specificity,

& yet all I can think of is debt & Martin,
never-ending childhood, anecdote, how sobriety

keeps me from saying anything I mean.
He spotted me outside the campus burrito barn,

coaxing my wallet from a bush beside
the parking lot, clutching an empty beer,

there was nothing for him to do.
Only small clouds here. Here, only

small rains & in the morning one body
lying marked by four traffic cones

on Prytania, way down 10, where Martin's
Solo cup now seems petrified, useless as

notebooks we press close as waves
        to our chests.

Two

Art School Applicant Name: Violet Ruth Shepherd, "Letti"

Date of Birth: August 17, 2009 (The moon's in my first house, where the emotional self is restless and sometimes disguises sensitivities by finding new ways to feel.)

Guardian(s): Rebecca Stewart-Shepherd, Chief Warrant Officer Anderson Blake Shepherd 4

Student Current Email Address: ladyofshallot22@gmail.com

Letti

(The Interview)

My dad's job in Afghanistan
was to pick guys up after mission.

He once made it outside Kandahar

before the propeller hit some trash
& this mattress cut off the leg of a soldier

he carried. When we studied Romeo and Juliet

I kept thinking, sometimes it's the Montagues
& the Capulets, sometimes it's a man against

a mattress. You're the guy who read

my story, right? You know how it opens
with a father watching this shooting star

from a living room window? In my head

it's not a star. In my head it's his kid hid
in a tin can, cannonballing through space.

We come from hill country,
Oregon, so after moving down here
I didn't get the birds. Waterfowl. Not my thing.

Like trying to love a language you can't speak. It was like
how people say the Koreas are making up but no one actually
believes it except those who believe it—there should be
   a name for that.

You Google the attack in Liege
& right square in the article is an ad
for the perfect maxi dress. Dumb, you know

it's dumb, but also consider asking Dad if you can
buy it for your mom since last you checked her search
history was all: beautiful actresses over 40, Julianne Moore age,

what is a flat white, are you my angel. Anyway,
   the birds here. All that water. It's like they depend
      on it. It's like a bad boyfriend. It's like some identity thing.

When I grow up I'm writing alone
on the Damariscotta River with a black dog—
friends say that's weird but think of the Polish chemist
Clara Immerwahr—first lady PhD in her field, married in Breslau.

It's hard to know what way to order
a story. Dad says *you only got so long*
to get in the boat. But you can't give it all away
up front either. Tricky business. The husband became

famous for swinging gas into warfare.
No stopping him. Money, recognition, she stayed
home with a baby. The soul has moments of escape but
only if you let it. Let me finish: When people ask why I don't

want kids I can't exactly say
because of some stupid Dickinson line—
because of some Polish chemist who shot herself in the heart.

How did you hear about our school? This older kid from my town came for dance but I think she got kicked out for vaping in a parking garage with her understudy.

Why would you like to attend our institution? Sometimes I'll see a word like *caribou* and wish I could spend the entire afternoon writing stories about a guy named Denis transporting caribou across Siberia. But also in the fourth grade my babysitter read this June Jordan poem aloud and I had to go lie down for a whole day but not in a bad way.

ZZ Packer, Raymond Carver, Zadie Smith.
        Barry Hannah, Larry Brown, may I look

at my notes? Junot Diaz, Jhumpa Lahiri,
        I saw on the website you don't want kids

who read sci fi, fantasy, old stuff. But
        Nat Geo just reported a lake on Mars.

Tell me that doesn't make you want
        to write some story about a pregnant

Mars-lady who recycles, yells to her
        other kids, *stop playing Fortnite*, falls

in love with the wrong guy across a lake.
        There's a way to live on another planet

        & y'all aren't into it?

Kayla in my creative writing class says
we write because we'd die if we didn't.

She's so small they made her cheer team
flier, I guess she's used to speaking for a group.

You die without water, for walking down
the wrong street, you die because you

were born in the wrong place, wrong color.
I know for a fact the only other available

elective was steel drums & the teacher yells.
Just saying, I have this heart thing, it doesn't

matter, but everyone calls it a condition,
Your condition. In my stories I don't have

a condition. In my stories people still
carry lunch pails, people still jump trains.

In the MRI machine, my father recites
Gay Chaps at the Bar while Mom & I wait

in another room, watching an episode of Vera
on her phone, reading one-pot recipes

from a years-old magazine. They want
to confirm a supreme court justice who's hurt

women, we think.

One of the lines in that poem goes,
But nothing ever taught us to be islands.

You know the neighborhood boys
are coming for someone when you can hear

their fun from down the street. Just in case
it's me, I always lie down under

the town widow's magnolia & try remembering
what words I know that make me want to keep awake.

Revision? Not sure what you mean.
No one reads my stories because what if
they said change this, & change this, lose this.
Before long I wouldn't recognize a thing I'd ever made.

You don't go performing plastic surgery
on a baby. My parents never sang any nursery
rhymes, but they read me this Yeats poem—it's tiny—
he makes his song a coat. You only make your songs coats

to take them outside. I don't do that. Outside's
where homeless cats are, & Jacob Lowry, & the world.

Do you have any concerns about the application? I guess since last year I made a C in geometry and then had this little freak-out in Honors Orchestra but not really besides that.

Aside from your chosen art area, what fields of study interest you? Those dogs the Russians sent up into space, paranormal activity, repurposing things. I really like Geometry a whole lot. The reason I did poorly with it was only because thinking about shapes got really overwhelming toward the end.

Weirdest thing I ever saw was a funeral
process through our apartment complex—lace
showcased across the hearse. They only ever come

through real neighborhoods, I thought.
You notice how the shoddier the buildings,
the nicer their names? Green Valley, Stonesthrow,

Lakeside Palace. They've all got
so much spring in them. I don't know
about the south just yet. Everyone seems really

nice. Everyone seems like they're going to sing
you a song or break into your closet dead of night,
steal the stray you keep hidden, its food, hell—even its blanket.

My friend Patrick says *no poems*
with cicadas in them, but also he's

one of those guys who only reads tomes.
So it's like: dude, you're fifteen. Try no

poems with the big words you use
to hide from everybody. He likes jazz

& he likes jazz for real, so I'm always
telling him, *just write jazz poems, Jesus.*

I say no poems with adjectives in them.
My third grade teacher called them sparkle

words, but all I ever care about are verbs.
Eccentric is easy. Try writing about

your bipolar aunt they found hitching
just south of Salem, holding one ice skate,

trying to find her way into the Enchanted Forest.

Boarding school scares me
because I've never had a roommate.
My mom wine reps for this Italian importer

& keeps case after case under the stairs. Sometimes
they leave me alone for entire days & I'm not even tempted

since I read once in the thirties Italians
broke bottles along advance lines so Ethiopian
soldiers, bootless, bled from the feet up. It's fucked.

Excuse me. Bullies. What I mean is I can't even eat
at the strip mall Tuscan place because the chef there beats

chicken breasts with bricks
before cooking them. Their being dead
already never stops my heart from breaking.

Five words that aptly describe yourself: Christmas frigatebird, affable, high-tide, decoupage*

*If you'll allow a sixth: portmanteau.

Early in *To Kill a Mockingbird*
it's summer's end & Dill's getting
on the train back to Meridian. Scout thinks,

I was miserable without him until it occurred to me
I'd be starting school in a week. Whatever that is, I'm that.

You seem nice, like a guy who wouldn't
want to look like a young Woody Allen
but happens to anyway. Are you a dad?

Mine once brought a snow globe back
from Oahu—inside's a cabana, an umbrella
with umbrellas painted on it. Funny, sure,

you couldn't not get the joke. But also
all the Bering Sea ice has melted. There's
so much I have that I don't want. As a kid

I squeezed myself between the washer
& dryer anytime I thought about infinity.
But maybe the opposite is worse. Other kids

must think like that. I have to think that's true.

Seventh grade school play they made us
all a state something—Valerie the Boykin Spaniel,
Terrell a Carolina wren (funny since he's got that shock

of white hair from a birthmark), they named me amethyst
though I've never worn jewelry a day in my life. It was May,

we'd lived here a month, I didn't understand why
all the moms seemed available at two in the afternoon.
I once had a babysitter who wanted to be a writer. She read

Larry Levis poems all the time. In this one, something *bothers*
a whole line of elms. For a while in everything I wrote one thing
   bothered

something else. It's like I'm always trying
things on. I don't want to be an artist like that.
People like that are how cults build followings. I'm not

a poet. I write stories. I couldn't make music if you paid me.
Think of the wren, though, how he trills an entire song in two
   seconds flat.

My plans are simple,
to farm blueberries up east—

They're tolerant. They like full sun.

I love school but
don't see myself going to college,
don't see myself going Army. I see

my grandfather fishing razor clams
in Agate Beach. They like brush, shallow

water. My grandfather liked his time,
he liked wading in only to his boot-tops.

You probably think of Mary Oliver
as a poet, but she's maybe best at journaling,

which Patrick says isn't really an art form
but my mom calls the guy who details her car

a genius, so it's like: perspective.
Field journals are my favorite thing.

Sometimes the notes you take far exceed
what you could ever create from them.

Sometimes as a kid I can only go
as far as the road, but even there

are riches: late morning when the sun
& moon stay out together, the metal

praying mantis Mr. Miller glued
to his mailbox, the photographer taking

engagement photos of a couple walking
straight down the middle of two yellow lines.

Three

Letter To Hannah From The Cafeteria During First Lunch At The Art School Where I Teach

2016

I just want Amy Poehler to be happy,
island-exiled & rich as that morning you arrived
  unprecisely edged in a black bathing suit & we lay

by the apartment pool reading translated Neruda
  & when we showed up at the foot of I no longer
  love her, that's certain, but maybe I love her

you squealed & the belly chain wearing you
  around the waist blazed like sometimes here
    the vocalists do & the ballet dancers but never

the cellists or—weird—the animation kids who
  carry their heroes around inside screens & slate gray
    portfolios. Anyway, she's split again, Amy, & I'm not

saying—perhaps this Us Weekly article isn't even saying—
  that a man has anything to do with anything, but how about
    the time you schlepped the hours-long drive to my duplex

carrying a case of cheap pink wine & an intro to Spanish CD
    stuck in your player converting You had been skinny, now
        you are fat, that couple is not using protection all the way

down I-95. I hid beneath the dining room table fisting
    hymnals of grass because the dining room table lived
        for a few bad nights after he left in the yard. Your man

had ridden a double-named girl along Carolina Beach
    Pier like a song nobody's ever cared about, same place
        where Billy Worthen once hummed When You Were Mine

thinking of another while I stripped upright on a yellow towel.
    Back then I let just about anyone have at me. The Pope, Michelle
        Obama, millions readying for mass on our school television

administration bought so that the student body can witness
    the closed caption of hell our country's in. Back when, that pope
        shoveled as a bouncer in a Buenos Aires club where someone

once blew a gun up my mother's dress. Think of all he could
    have done but didn't. I want to be at work on a poem when I die.
        The same night whitening the same trees. I want it to be like that.

Before you broke came the book you wrote & in it
  a son & in it the mean snow & on hot days I carry them both
    around in my belly instead of you. My father's dying, which is why

I'm writing, which is why at 11:11 I kiss the face of my iPhone
  to un-die him. He's a globe, he's a night-light in the shape of a conch,
    he thinks this election might kill him worse than what'll kill him.

Which is the weight of what we keep asking of him,
  which is to stay alive. Which is what I'm asking of you
    as well. It's all selfishness over here, like any letter

that has nothing, really, to do with the beloved. I want you
  alive. I want you stitching all the frayed hairs on my head
    into a single smart wreath, making promises the way all

girl children do when they're alone just
  before a man comes in to switch off the lights.

Everyone I've Danced With Is Dead.

It's the summer we think our father's new breathing machine might
change the world, the summer my thirty year-old sister reads a book

all the way through for the first time, the June some umpire tells
a man he's safe when he isn't, then cries about it to all the newspapers.

We've rented a beach house with all our money. A plane flies over,
carrying letters proposing to Rita across an impossible sky.

My nephew is five & already wants to know the dormant story
of every besieged city in the world. He calls this beach his beach.

He calls this house, his house. The sky, any species of bee,
the three words in another language he's learned—there's nothing

that doesn't belong to him. Me? I'm scared of everything,
even drunks outside ice cream shops, even the plovers flying

scary-low, as if they actually want another hero's waves all over them.

Everyone I've Danced With Is Dead.

Lent, 1993, & Chris Webber ousts a time-out
that doesn't exist, some wrong airplane of his brain
cocked & lifting off, all of Michigan snapping shut

inside their shame. Sixth grade, Brady Kent
sometimes still pees herself during our adolescent
nasturtiums of laughter. No one's come up dead

yet. I smoke so many things & hardly inhale any
of them. What does it matter. We're rooting for
the other, southern team alongside all our fathers.

Bells ring us in for supper after day-long games
of manhunt. My sister gives up eating, but evenings
an angel straps her down, feeds her dry cereal

from a Solo cup. Us girls want to protect each other
but we don't know how. We hide face-up under trees.
We think our insipid anger might just be enough.

Everyone I've Danced With Is Dead.

When this six-top of college girls orders a pitcher
of sangria, it's likely some gateway drug to rebellion
in this Christian college town—they're twenty-something

& still earn demerits for sitting cross-legged or trafficking
the sidewalk kept sacred for men. I'm seventeen & have been
a waitress for one thousand years. The varsity defensive line dubs

me Flaming Virgin. We devil-stick. We hacky-sack up
& down third period study hall. We're so proud of ourselves.
It's 1999. I close the Irish pub after working a double with so much

Grateful Dead on loop. Oz the line cook asks me back to his place
for beers & lets me out of his closet three days later. The light's so
bright all I understand is a tattoo of waves crashing over one bony hip.

When I'm little Dad recites *Ode on a Grecian Urn* every time
we go out for one of his brick-laying jobs. I'm in charge of mortar.
I love the bit about the bride so stuck in time she can never get caught.

Tale Of Two Line Cooks

I.

Mi maestra, I am
too stupid for a wife, he says.

Then, as if to explain,
rolls a single pant leg

to unearth a traveling song
of scars. *One night, all the men*

on my side of Guatemala
told me not to run, & I ran.

II.

There are days when I feel more
equipped scrubbing sunchokes

than teaching the sacrifice
of Iphigenia to seventh grade

prep school kids up the road,
how brave it was she knew

whatever place. Days I clock in
so tired Celso assumes I've been up

all night fucking. *Squeaky-squeaky,*
he says, mock-humping the co2 tank

in dry storage like we both don't sleep
on mattresses that lie flat against a floor.

He goes back to shaving four hundred
garlic cloves against the blade of mandolin,

a tied superhero mask of restaurant-grade
plastic wrap around his head to protect

the eyes. I go back to scrawling
today's date in Sharpie across

the wide chest of quart containers.
We laugh a laugh that sets just enough

rules on fire to fulfill the sweet tooth
of resentment, which makes a mockery

of almost anything.

III.

The first year I asked
how he came into this country

Celso said, *I travel by bus
you stupid slut.* Vos ramera

torpe. The fourth year
I asked he said, *We walked.*

*We passed skeletons lying
facedown still wearing*

*their backpacks. All the things
inside were gone: apples & water,*

all of our shy-mouthed sisters.

Everyone I've Danced With Is Dead.

The flowers begin to arrive right away:

mansions of white roses, blooming twig trophies.

My husband's hosing off the side porch. Sister's at church

figuring out music Dad might want. Some man emerges

from this gray van carrying a lit cigarette in one hand, vase

in another, asks if I'm my mother & I sign for it like I am.

Wait, he says, *didn't we work together way back?* We don't

give enough credit to kindness, to time. I almost don't recall

the closet or anything that happened inside. From the knee down

instead of a right leg he's got a metal rod. *Bet you're wondering*

what happened there. The hose runs so steadily you can't hear it.

Drunk driver hit me head on. Took everything from me

 in a single second.

Everyone I've Danced With Is Dead.

In the dream my husband's ex-wife suggests
we go in together on a pyramid scheme selling

chocolates & it feels like high school in a good way,
we're lying in the hay of a barn loft with just enough

room to put a person between us. In real life
she left for Oregon harvest & never came back.

I like to imagine her squishing grapes barefooted
in coveralls, feeling light. Once, when she was

the wife & I their waitress, she invited me
to a party & for favors handed out cacti tucked

inside hand-painted pots. I went to pee & fell in love
with their shower curtain—embroidered beasts

the color of wheat--& when I moved in ten years
later it was all she'd left. When my buddy Chris

OD'd behind the Bojangles I meant to quit work,
drop my pit Henrietta at a friend's, drive west

to Big Sur or at least Montgomery & never return.
But I had a shift that night running patio with M'Randa.

It was warm, clear—I wouldn't do M'Randa like that.
The dream ends all abrupt because my mom calls

in the thirty-minute window she has to be alive
inside her own body while my father nebulizes.

I've been reading this Mary Oliver poem about stones.
I say, *Watering the Stones?* & she says:

  No, just plain old lonesome Stones.

The Spare Room

Story goes when Lindsey Buckingham gave up
water polo, his high school coach yelled,

You're a loser, & you'll always be a loser,

is what I'm telling you over fried chicken & German wine
the waiter said tasted of almond & does, unlike the verdejo

I said resembled, in flavor, grass, to the customer sucking a
toothpick

who returned with, *Lady, does it look like
I got out of bed this morning to drink
some fucking grass?*

Which managed to dethrone my sadness

for a couple minutes before the lady at 21 yelled—
as if on fire—*My poached egg arrived ruptured!*

I arrive most places ruptured, also apologetic,
wrecking the formula of more geese-gliding folk.

The article suggesting we visit Ontario refers to

    the antique poetry of life,

which I can't quit chanting, all soft, while cleaning
probiotic smoothie from our pitbull's shnozz, she who

adores licking the dishwasher's bottom rack
    while I load the top. Poetry used to make up

    the entire board game of my vocabulary,

but I've read enough undergrad drafts to know
just how many of us grubby kids stole change

from atop the dresser of whatever adult
    was for the most part keeping us alive.

In dreams I'm married to plenty of people,
none of whom are you:

> McCauley Culkin's first cousin,
> a former student who wrote entirely
> of Tiffany lamps, Jeff from college.

In the Zoom session I agreed to host on romance,
people wanted to know some tips on how to write

about a partner, but shit if I've ever penned a thing.
I think often of your sad years living

in that couple's spare room, before Iraq,
with only your bedframe & 5$ Subway & pull-up bar,

> that Army Bible Study you led called *The Navigators*.

Story goes, story goes, story goes—
In therapy Carla says: *Jesus, can't you tell me*

something from childhood that's not a fucking narrative?

Carla says: *Okay, so the goal is for you to become more*

    like Nancy Pelosi.

She thinks if we sit very still & for a long time our childhood
will wash over us, visual as film, free as fish.

She thinks we shouldn't be so scared of swimming.

After reading Maggie Nelson's book about her murdered aunt,
all any of the students wanted to discuss was what right did she have

going through a dead person's journals. How like this century
the whole talk went.

   Wasn't it Auden who said, *& ghosts must do again*
     what gives them pain?

The night they rushed Dad to ICU for the final time
was my first sleeping at your place, so I showed up

at the hospital in a crop top & fancy blue flares,
  which was all I had,
    which made everyone laugh for a second or two.

Sometimes I remember the shit beach house we rented
after lockdown, how you heard the ice cream truck coming,
jumped down two flights of stairs in your red crab swimming trunks,

waited patient with your ten-dollar bill. I wanted to talk with you
through a tin can & string. You looked so protected standing there,

almost like a boy, almost like how safe we could've turned out
if we'd known each other sooner, like from the very beginning.

Everyone I've Danced With Is Dead.

after Sophie Young

Even winners can die, reports the headlines
& in the supporting role of photograph half

a dozen ball-capped men shower Arcadius
with bags of keg party ice. It's 2012.

I'm three months pregnant. The dad's bought
me a black-stoned ring from Dixie Gem while

his real girlfriend labors across town & all I crave
are buttered green beans topped with slivered

almonds my mother served some Easters.
I haven't even miscarried in the den of a party

& apologized for it yet. Sophia is ten &
won't become my favorite student for years.

She's never written a poem where the horse dies
on all her televisions & a kid in her class snorts

so much pixy stick she's sent snotting orange
to the nurse. The poem's about what we can

hotwire, more about what we can't. The last line
goes something like:

    It's been an unusual year for the girls.

Acknowledgments

Thank you to the following editors and publications in which some of these poems first appeared:

"Everyone I've Danced With Is Dead. (B's failing poetry)." *Fish Barrel Review.* 2021.

"Letter To Yasha In My Third Period AP Lang Class, Morning After That Girl She Likes Blocked Her On Instagram." *Four Way Review.* 2016.

"Everyone I've Danced With Is Dead (I don't know how to build the world)." *Washington Square Review.* 2021.

"Everyone I've Danced With Is Dead (The students have written about birds)." *Glass.* 2020.

"Everyone I've Danced With Is Dead (Hours before they identify him)." *Nimrod.* 2021.

"Bail" (under a different title). *Carolina Quarterly.* 2011.

"An excerpt of Letti." *The Yalobusha Review.* 2019.

"Letter To Hannah From The Cafeteria During First Lunch At The Boarding School Where I Teach." *Smartish Pace.* 2017.

"Everyone I've Danced With Is Dead (It's the summer we think)." *Fish Barrel Review.* 2021.

"Tale Of Two Line Cooks." *Muzzle.* 2016.

"Everyone I've Danced With Is Dead (*Even winners can die*)." *Fish Barrel Review.* 2021.

It begins and ends with my dad, who thankfully parented with poetry when other modes of communication felt too elusive. Yeats, Nina Simone, Keats, Etheridge Knight. How I wish you were earthside to see a book finally come to fruition. Look Pop! I made my song a coat!

Many thanks to Mark Cox who taught me how to read poems and, more importantly, how to be kind to them. Mark, if I had the words for you, I'd use them, but the trailhead you led me to is beyond vocabulary.

Much of this book is a reaching toward friends who are no longer with us. I'd give all the poetry in the world for them to be here instead.

I was lucky enough to teach creative writing for nearly fifteen years at South Carolina's Governor's School for the Arts and Humanities. It was the single honor of my life, and Letti is dedicated to that honor. I've learned more from students than they likely ever learned from me. I extend my gratitude eternally to the class of 2021. You are every levitating Arcade Fire song. You are that fist-to-the-chest Future Islands moment when they performed on Letterman.

This collection is dedicated to poets Kirby Knowlton and to Patrick Whitfill. They sent edits. They sent poems. They sent memes. They kept me alive inside this book. And thank you, of course, to JackLeg for thinking that this could be a book at all.

I won't bore you with how much I love my husband, Alan, because there's a whole other collection of poems out there dedicated to him.

Thank you to the rest of our family: Mom, Molly, Morgan, and Luke. Thank you to my dear friend Sangeeta who said, "I'm going to buy a lot of your books, but I might not ever read them." Thank you to Ashley Warlick, who reads every early, manic rough draft and pretends to like all of them. Thank you to every restaurant manager who's ever given me a job, particularly the ones who also offered health insurance. A thousand bows to Chris George for giving me a place to live for a few months, and for allowing me to stay five years. A thousand bows to Alan Rossi for being a good, good man. Thank you Hannah and Daisy and Stevie and McSween and Bill and Vith and the rest of our MFA crew. Gratitude, really, to anyone who lives among us while we try to create.

My final and most important bow goes to our dogs, Henrietta Modine and Wednesday Stewart. Retta sat by my side while I wrote most of this. We love each other when we're fearless, when we're scared shitless. Thankful to both for loving me whether I write a single line, or don't.

JACKLEG PRESS

V. Joshua Adams, Scott Shibuya Brown, Brian Rivka Clifton, Brittney Corrigan, Jessica Cuello, Barbara Cully, Alison Cundiff, Neil de la Flor, Suzanne Frischkorn, Victoria Garza, Reginald Gibbons, Joachim Glage, Caroline Goodwin, Kathryn Kruse, Meagan Lehr, Brigitte Lewis, Jenny Magnus, D.K. McCutchen, Jean McGarry, Rita Mookerjee, Mamie Morgan, Alexis Orgera, Karen Rigby, Jo Salas, Maureen Seaton, Kristine Snodgrass, Cornelia Maude Spelman, Peter Stenson, Melissa Studdard, Curious Theatre, Gemini Wahhaj, Megan Weiler, Cassandra Whitaker, David Wesley Williams

jacklegpress.org